Step Zero: Getting Started
A SCUBA Photo Trip

Dennis Adams   *Cathy Swan*   *Peter Swan*

Step Zero: Getting Started on
A SCUBA Photo Trip

Published by Lulu.com
dr-swan@cox.net

ISBN 978-1-4357-1533-2

Printed in the United States of America

TABLE OF CONTENTS

PREFACE

This book is a project of love. We are all SCUBA divers from the middle of the last century and photographers from longer ago than that. Having migrated from local diving to the new era of global travelers we are recording our adventures underwater. We have acquired skills necessary to conduct Underwater Photo Safaris through years of trial and error. Our motivation for the book occurred as our friends asked the basic, and not so basic, questions:

How do you prepare for a global Underwater Photo Safari?
How do you begin the initial "Step Zero?"

The ease of our approach seemed to be natural; but, further discussions showed that many people were overwhelmed with the initial steps necessary to begin an Underwater Photo Safari. This book came about when we realized that the skills we have developed over the years could be easily explained and documented enabling "first-timers" to confidently pursue the actions that lead to a great trip with fun and games under water.

Arrow Crab in Sponge
Pentax Optio S5i, 5 megPix
Flash: auto   Settings: Auto

Our concept is that if you can start properly, the rest falls into place. As a result, we have come up with the concept of "Step Zero" [How does one start planning for a trip?] as the basis of our book. This very preliminary phase of the process is emphasized throughout this book - along with other steps outlined to ensure everyone can pull together a complex project in a timely manner and make the decisions necessary to succeed in a seemingly simple process. Thus, the Step Zero method.

We call this effort Book One of our series as it is the first where we actually went on a trip using the checklist process. This trip to Grenada spanned ten days with stays at the True Blue Bay Resort prior to and after our 7 day Underwater Photo Safari on Peter Hughes' Wind Dancer. Our "proof testing" of the Step Zero process on a series of trips will lead to future books based upon our successes or failures.

We would like to thank the Peter Hughes dive operations team for their special treatment over our many charters with them. Of course, all the other divers receive the same treatment, so "special to all" is routine on a Peter Hughes boat. The Grenada Wind Dancer crew was especially helpful with the little things such as getting in and out of the dive tenders. The islands that we sailed around are shown on the next page. In addition, we would like to show our love of our families as they support us on our many travel adventure excursions. Sometimes they join us and sometimes we must explore on our own. We love it when they join us and we love them even when we are away. What a privilege to be able to indulge ourselves while traveling the world on Underwater Photo Safaris. Rick Larned was not on any of our team trips; but, is a friend of long standing who understands the difficulty of starting a project. He helped us understand the need for the Step Zero process by suggesting the name. Thanks Rick!

Map of the area where the boat sailed. [1]

---

[1] Peter Hughes Diving website, Granada Wind Dancer, 1 April 2008.

CHAPTER 1:   INTRODUCTION – YOUR GUIDE TO PREPARATION FOR AN UNDERWATER PHOTO SAFARI

The Step Zero process helps you understand the basics of... Where to go? When to go? How to go? And who to go with? Chapter 1 lays out the process to follow while preparing for the adventure associated with an Underwater Photo Safari. Hopefully, it is straightforward and not intimidating. For the "first timers," this book will layout a process that can be followed to enable you to go from the basic desire to the actual event without too much stress. For the "old-timers," this may be a process to augment your personal trip planning methods to ensure success.

Wind Dancer
Pentax Optio S5i,
5 megPix
Flash:auto
Settings: auto
Distance: auto

LEVERAGE THE EXCITEMENT

The excitement of the first morning on the Underwater Photo Safari is special -- even after the stimulation of a few days of global travel beforehand. The exhaustion is overcome by the newness and expectations.

The realization that you are going on an adventure; recognition of a new location to play within; fun of exploring unknown depths; and, "expectations of a lifetime" are all realized during the week(s) on the chosen trip. The building of excitement is tempered with the knowledge that you are indulging yourself in a life-long dream. Excitement is the word that conveys the feelings that we have every time we set up one of these trips and plan for months with friends to investigate the myriad of choices. Each time we commit to an Underwater Photo Safari, we feel emotions that must be similar to the historic wanderers of the world; explorers, vagabonds, wealthy hunters, adventurers and movers. Thank goodness for air travel cutting these trips down to reasonable travel times of days and weeks versus months or years. New places, people, experiences, and a variety of underwater fish/flora/fauna ensure an adventure every time. Throughout the book, memorable events are highlighted in boxes. The dimension of photography makes it even more enjoyable when you can bring home the "fish stories" to share with friends and family. Why do we go? Because we can, and must, investigate over the hill and under the water.

This book is about the very real problem of how to go about refining your thoughts into a plan that can be executed toward a SCUBA trip of a lifetime. The decisions are serial and all interrelated upon themselves. Examples of each of the major phases of the plan will be shown with explanations and pictures. The essence of this book is that a weeklong Underwater Photo Safari is rewarding, surprising, and just plain fun – if well planned. As we go through the phases of the Step Zero process we will use the example of our trip to Grenada and the Peter Hughes boat, Wind Dancer, in October 2007. We have found that one of the major issues people face in a Underwater Photo Safari is that they do not know where to start; nor, how to pull together the trip details to ensure that the pain is minimized and the pleasure is maximized. So, here is how you do it! This book will help you answer the following questions.

- What things do I need to know to go on an Underwater Photo Safari?
- What do I do first?
- How do I get there from here?
- How do I approach dive buddies?
- Do I have the training required?
- Do I need new equipment

LEVERAGE THE STEP ZERO PROCESS

Many first timers find the process too complex to even begin; as the world is large, the choices varied, and the feedback confusing. This consternation is the reason the book focuses upon the initial phases of the adventure while showing all the steps and processes we have developed to have a productive, and memorable, trip – for all the right reasons. The basic concept revolves around Step Zero.

Step Zero: The establishment of initial
and consistent thoughts toward a goal.

	"How To" Guide
Premise	Preparation – Preparation – Preparation [guidebook: Pre-travel, trip activities, post travel]
Focus	International travel [with example of Grenada] Underwater Photo Safari – boat or land based
Includes	Timelines, what to do (and not do), checklists, what to take (and what to leave behind)
Goal	Provide you with confidence as you leave your doorstep on an international Underwater Photo Safari [ensure nuisances do not become catastrophic events]

One example of a key thing to remember in this silly world of airlines and transportation is that you cannot always expect your bags to show up when and where you do. It is, therefore, necessary to plan on getting to your final location at least two days prior to initiation of the official SCUBA diving trip. This means that you have to plan on airline, hotels, and transportation to mesh with the departure date and time of your SCUBA activities. This is especially important if your Underwater Photo Safari is based upon a live aboard as the boat usually leaves the area and does not return until the next week. In that case, it is imperative that you show up two days early and book into a nice hotel close to the departure arena [usually coordinated with the boat team]. These spare days allow time for your luggage to catch up, for you to see the local culture, and to recover from your jet lag.

Spotted Moray Eel
Pentax Optio S5i,
5 megPix
Flash: auto
Settings: auto
Distance: auto

CHAPTER LAYOUT

This book is laid out to be used as a template for your trip with an identifiable process and a complete checklist to make certain you do not forget necessary actions or items. The Step Zero process is shown below with the chapter descriptions following. The authors hope this sets the stage for an exciting Underwater Photo Safari.

Step Zero Process - Your Guide to Preparation

Step & Chapter	Process Name
1	Introduction – Your Guide to Preparation - Underwater Photo Safari
2	Long-Range Preparation [Planning, planning, and more planning]
3	Mid-Range Preparation
4	Week Prior Preparation
5	Concurrent Activities & Planning [land based or live aboard]
6	Preparing for Photographic Activities
7	Trip Completion Preparation

INTRODUCTION TO CHECKLIST

The Step Zero process depends upon the ability to plan and prepare for the trip. SCUBA diving requires a lot of equipment; therefore, there must be a method that enables you to bring all the necessary items -- as there are no stores after you leave the dock and, many times, not at the dock either. Over many years of diving and going on Underwater Photo Safaris, we have developed a series of checklists for international trips that can ensure you do not leave essential elements at home or forget to purchase them when you are at your destination. The checklist enables the prospective traveler to ensure that proper equipment has been loaded into the bags. It is made up of two classes of ideas; ***ACTIONS*** that we need to accomplish and ***EQUIPMENT*** checklists that recognize essential items for the trip. Action items are things you should accomplish during the preparation phases while the equipment checklist makes sure you have purchased, maintained, and prepared the necessary items for the trip.

1. Action Items
   - Team Based
   - Individual Actions

2. Equipment Checklist
   - Individual
   - Shared
   - Backup

In addition, this Underwater Photo Safari checklist breaks items into long-term, mid-term and short-term preparation. This allows you the opportunity to plan for, purchase the essential items, train for the event, and pack for the desired trip of a lifetime. A fully consolidated checklist is shown in its full glory in the appendix in a manner that can be used for future trips. As evidenced from our recent trip to Grenada, even having the checklist, some things are still forgotten. This mandates that we actually USE the checklist.

Memorable Events   **Forgotten Cards**

There are many reminders in the checklist to bring along your proof of SCUBA certification, training, and expertise. On our trip to Grenada, Pete left them all at home. Fortunately, he had a day prior to boarding the boat (as we always recommend) and his wife (loving and understanding) was home to fax them to him. Do not forget your SCUBA cards.

In addition to the two major sections of the checklist, there are four categories of essential items that must not be forgotten or left behind.

1. Money: Check books, credit cards, ATM cards, cash in all denominations
2. Must take dive documents: SCUBA certification cards, Dan ID and medical insurance card, and NITROX certification.
3. Must take travel documents: Passport (with visas), airline tickets, diver resort confirmation, drivers license, hotel confirmations, immunization certification, medical insurance cards, trip itinerary
4. Medicine: Whatever is necessary for your health while away from your corner drugstore

The following is a *small extract* from the full checklist shown in the appendix.

ACTIONS you must do

	Completed
Long-Term Actions	
L book your vacation days at work	_____
Medium-Term Actions	
M arrange care for animals/pets/lawn/flowers	_____
Short-Term Actions	
S call credit card companies, tell them you are going overseas so they may adjust your spending profile	_____
Action Things to do ON the trip	
call your dive tour company and let them know you have arrived in the vacation area and will be at the appropriate location for pick up as scheduled.	_____

Action Things to do at the END of the trip

buy replacement or upgrade to better equipment   _____

Action Things to NOT do/take on the trip

scuba tanks, they are very heavy and provided by
most scuba operations as part of your dive charter   _____

EQUIPMENT Check List

Dive Equipment
Basic Equipment
M-buoyancy compensation device   _____
Safety Equipment
M-chemical/cyalume light stick   _____
Backup Equipment

Photography
L-Land Camera (are you going to take one)   _____
L-Under Water (UW) camera (are you going to take one)   _____

NOTES: _____

_____

_____

_____

CHAPTER 2: LONG-RANGE PREPARATION

This chapter lays out the essential elements of the long-range preparation and planning so the pre-trip activities follow a path that will lead to a successful adventure. There are many varied activities that take time and must be accomplished well before departure. Each of them may seem intimidating, unless you break them down into easy steps and process sequentially. Some highlights of the items this chapter will emphasize are:

- Make a commitment to go, -- where & when
- Location choice
- Passport check
- Airline reservations
- Review a total checklist
- What type of training
- What photographic equipment
- Team party

Banded Reef Shrimp
Pentax Optio S5i,
5 megPix
Flash: auto
Settings: auto
Distance: macro

START THE PROCESS: ASK QUESTIONS

The fun of traveling for SCUBA photography makes the trials and tribulations worthwhile. We have enjoyed SCUBA for over 40 years and have developed a great feel for the photographic aspects of the sport. We will show a methodology that has worked for us and layout process steps that will enable the reader to make sure the right activities happen in the right order with the right priority. When traveling with a group, you many want to have one person do the travel planning for those who may find the task too intimidating. The examples shown in this book will come from the Grenada live aboard Underwater Photo Safari. In our group, there was one person who was an excellent diver, but could not plan. We had to ensure that he got to the restaurants for dinner and then tell him what to do and when to be ready for doing it. Some people excel at planning while some enjoy the excitement of random events.

It is amazing the confusion you experience when you decide that you want to go on an international Underwater Photo Safari. You experience thousands of questions and multiple choices to fulfill your dreams. The bottom line of our special approach is: Preparation - Preparation - Preparation. Some of the early planning steps include:

- Chose a location and time frame [month or season]
- Print out maps of the area [hotels & dive areas]
- Ensure passport/visa are valid
- Learn about the country [politics, time zones, immigration, wet/dry season, currency exchange, State Department information]
- Learn about dive locations [go to the web and Travelin' Diver's Chapbook[2]]
- Initiate reservations

This leads one to the conclusion that you want to change the questions into answers for the group. We have laid out a column in the series of questions so that you may write down answers for your upcoming trip. This should help you prepare for the adventure.

---

[2] Davison, Ben. The 2008 Travelin' Diver's Chapbook, Undercurrent, 2008.

First Tier Questions

Questions	Possible Answers	Your Answers For New Trip
What do I want to do?	Live an adventure in a new place Go SCUBA diving with friends Record with photography	
Should I go on a boat or land dive?	Commit to full week + Need night life Seasick vs. robust at sea	
Should I go local or to a distant shore?	Live aboard and boat lifestyle Land based flexibility Level/type of diving desired Cold water vs. warm Short adventure or excursion Visit exotic locations	
How do I get there?	Depends on where and how much you want to spend; air vs. automobile, which airlines fly to which destination	
Where do I stay?	This takes research- Interim stops must be planned: Hotel vs. rental property Land dive program and/or location prior/after live aboard	

It turns out that our policy of "coordinated planning with individual execution" has worked very well and ensured that when things happen [oops did not get correct day reserved at hotel!] there is no one to blame but yourself. This creates much less tension within the trip participants. However, this does require excellent communication skills within the travel group.

"Coordinated Planning – Individual Execution."

Group Consensus	Individual Needs	Your Answers for New Trip
After group consensus, all trip partners make all arrangements themselves	Airlines and hotels Medicines/shots (malaria?) Special diet Equipment choices Camera equipment Computer support	

In addition, you must ask more detailed questions as a team and as an individual. Here are a series of "second tier questions" that we ask as we go forward in our planning.

Second Tier Questions

Questions	Possible Answers	Your Answers For New Trip
Now that I have picked a place (Grenada), how do I go about planning for that trip?	The planning process takes time and research. The beauty is that there is plenty of information on websites. The process must be sequential; however, as you proceed, the diversity of choices must be reviewed and narrowed to an achievable goal.	
Time of year for trip	When can you get time off What about hurricane and other weather related issues Availability of resort or boat	
Fly to where from where?	This is a major issue for all of us. We have to plan our trips around the availability of such things a "cheap" airline tickets or free tickets from our flight programs.	
And then of course... Lodging:	After the travel plan is in place [usually needs to be accomplished first and at least 6 months ahead of schedule], the lodging must be researched next. For live aboards, the planning must have you arriving at boat departure locations two days early to allow for potentially delayed baggage or buddies. Some buddies need lots of TLC.	
Who should plan and commit	Many groups/families have one person coordinate everything and commit for all. This approach works well; but, demands acceptance of another person's actions. Our group has a policy of: "coordinated planning with individual execution."	

Feather Duster Tube Worm
Pentax Optio S5i,
5 megPix
Flash: auto
Settings: Auto

Another key is early decision making. Although this is not essential as you can go at a drop of a snorkel and still have fun. We are believers in timely decisions and the enjoyment of planning. As such, we normally make the location decision a year ahead to ensure availability and reasonably priced airline tickets. Early planning and the willingness to make joint decisions inside the dive team leads to excellent preparation. One of our secrets is that we love to have our dive buddies meet periodically to show the images from the last trip and plan for the next trip. Planning, for us, is fun in and of itself – almost as good as kids anticipating their birthday. During the planning phase, there are many issues and discussions that occur. By planning early with good communications, the group can maximize their interaction effectiveness while ensuring not too much pain to any one individual. The final decision to go does not have to be made until you are ready to depart for the airport. Of course, there are financial impacts when you cancel late in the planning process. Some key elements of this early preparation include the following major activities:

- Can you take vacation from work?
- Determine location and timing
- Have a dive team gathering /party – periodically to review issues
- Make airline reservations
- Review total checklist and determine areas to fill in
- Determine if extra SCUBA training is required [open water, NITROX, deep diving, wreck diving, dive master]
- Start analyzing types of photography [above ground and under water with small version and/or complex larger camera apparatus]

Another long-term planning item is the possession of a passport and/or necessary visas for specific countries. The increase in security this century has resulted in changes around the world in passport control. In the United States, the Western Hemisphere Travel Initiative has required passports for far more travel locations enjoyed by SCUBA divers. It is very easy (and not too expensive) to acquire a passport; however, it does require time. If you think you might need one, it is worth going ahead and acquiring one for you and your traveling buddies. There are two items of importance once you have your passports: 1- make color copies – leave one behind with a relative or friend and bring one in separate luggage location, and 2 – protect the passport in a water repellent case (zip lock bags work well).

The next table shows the example of our trip to Grenada while answering some of the difficult questions.

Pre-Trip	Grenada Example (our answers for Oct 07 trip)	Your Answers
Commit to investigate going on an Underwater Photo Safari	Yes or No estimate on desire to participate from all potential members of the trip – preliminary answers June 07.	
Informally gather potential trip partners in a communications group	Create an email group(Jan 07): 8 + potential trip members to Grenada – kept throughout the trip preparation to share the adventure	
Discuss the timing with your potential trip partners	Spring 07 preliminary Yes Summer 07 final count, Fall 07 information to all	
Identify Locations of Choice - Boat vs. Land diving	Granada, Belize, Bahamas, Cayman, or Bermuda – Peter Hughes boats or land based hotels – Picked Wind Dancer Feb 07	
Decide on when and where to go for the Underwater Photo Safari	Decision was made at dive party in Feb 07 for an Oct 07 trip	
Investigate travel alternatives to the chosen destination	Direct to Grenada or overnight in San Juan/Miami (one choice) Hotels in Grenada	
Trade various factors with trip partners, initiate early decisions such as; location, timing, duration of trip, how many, pre/post trip activities	Planned to meet at chosen destination 2 or 3 days early to ensure dive equipment shows up. In Grenada, True Blue Resort for two nights prior and one night post boat trip around a seven day live aboard choice	

CHECKLIST FOR LONG-RANGE PLANNING

Long-Term Actions	**Completed**

L take vacation from work   _____

L add luggage catch up days to your travel plan, some
luggage will get lost on the airlines. A rest day will give it a   _____
chance to catch up with you.   _____

L make airline reservations   _____

L make hotel reservations

L make dive resort reservations

L passport expiration date; check it and ensure you will   _____
have at least 6 months left when you enter your
vacation area, more is better

L read lessons learned from your last trip   _____

L rest days, put them in your travel plan. This will give your   _____
body a chance to catch up and for you to see the
local area and enjoy your adventure

L time zones: do you cross the international date line?   _____
Watch this, you can loose or gain one day; this
can screw up your travel plans if you don't anticipate.

L dive trip planning parties; get together with friends   _____
and discuss going on a trip; medium term parties will
check individual progress and provide group support

NOTES: _____

_____

_____

_____

CHAPTER 3:   MID-RANGE PREPARATION

This time frame might seem to be one of easily proceeding toward an adventure; however, this is not true. This mid-range planning stage is where the "heavy hitting" must occur. Many items take time to order and cannot be acquired during the last week prior to the trip (such as hard to get lenses or specific dive computers). In addition, it takes time to get into shape with exercise. New training consumes much time also, so if you want to be NITROX trained, start early. There are two levels of getting ready for an Underwater Photo Safari, emotional and equipment.

The key to the emotional level is that it is very complex at many levels when interfacing with many people on multiple issues. The next emotional factor is the recognition of the excitement and expectation of friends on adventures. The group level interfacing is dynamic with feedback on which airline, which cities, and which time schedules. Group solutions to the multiple emotional issues require complex feedback and detail.

- Emotional Level
    - Travel Team Level: This involves the element of communications and commitment. Plans must be accomplished in a positive and timely manner. A week together should start out with a exciting "vibe" inside the travel team, which starts with planning.
    - Individual Level: Key personal elements of preparation include training [level of SCUBA expertise and physical preparation], proper planning for trip [check on airline, reserve hotels and cars, update visa/passports], and commitments reference work schedules and personal obligations.

The second recognition of things to accomplish in this mid-range period is based around the hardware and equipment. There are many various types of equipment and functions that have to be achieved during the Underwater Photo Safari. One item that we all notice with other divers is the need to have the "wow factor" with their equipment. The biggest, the best and the most sophisticated.

- Equipment Level: This involves acquiring the proper equipment for the trip; training for its use; practice to ensure the equipment and person work well together; and, are all the pieces available, with backup parts. One key item is batteries... buy early, charge up often, check prior to trip, and charge again. In addition, check for battery disposal regulations in the area you are going to visit.

EMOTIONAL LEVEL PREPARATION

Travel Team Level: This activity involves the element of communications and commitment. Nothing is worse than having the whole team cancel on you after you are packed and ready to go. Plans must be accomplished that ensure the travel team meets at certain locations and are responsible for certain parts of the team's activities. A week on an Underwater Photo Safari should start out with a positive "vibe" inside the group. A "win-win" relationship must be developed among the total travel team. Continuous emails work well as a mechanism to keep everyone informed.

After the long-range decisions are made, each participant must now ensure that their plans are progressing as they needed them to progress. At this level it involves the key elements of preparation [including training], proper planning for trip [purchase airline, reserve hotels and cars, gain visa/passports], and commitment [reference work and personal schedules]. With the concept of "coordinated planning – individual execution," communications between trip members is important. The preparation during this mid-range period is sporadic; but, you must keep checking your status. Keep asking "Did I forget an important step or item?" Solutions to multiple issues require complex feedback and detailed discussions with the travel team to ensure solutions match the circumstances. Peer pressure with constant feedback ensures the whole is working toward a common solution. Frequent coordination through multiple parties, emails and phone calls leads to excellent communications and helps (but does not guarantee) everyone stays on budget and schedule.

Memorable Events   Extra Night in Puerto Rico

On the Grenada trip we soon realized that Pete had to have an extra night in Puerto Rico instead of going directly to the boat location in Grenada. In this trip planning, he needed an extra travel day as the combination of inexpensive airline ticket and connections did not match up. Others were able to make the trip from Virginia to Grenada in one day to enable two buffer days of rest and preparation. The Peter Hughes Dive travel shop had booked him for two evenings at the True Blue Bay Resort prior to the dive boat departure. However, the airline was not able to ensure that he arrived in Granada on time. As a result, his agent booked him an overnight stay in Puerto Rico and only one night in Granada. The mid-range planning had all been accomplished; but, with the help of his dive buddies, he realized there was a disconnect in his planning. This led Pete to only having one day to spare at the boat location instead of two nights. This was OK as it still enabled him to have a spare day for the bag delivery with an intermediate check in Puerto Rico.

Individual Level: One of the key elements that should NOT be left until the last moment is the realization that you should be in good physical shape for multiple dives a day. As such, the training program should be multiple months long. In addition to physical strength and endurance training, expertise development is important. This mid-time period is excellent for more photography training and/or more SCUBA training. Some photography practice could deal with MACRO, wide-angle, high speed, wide aperture, or flash. Some excellent expertise leveraged on a Underwater Photo Safari would be NIRTOX, open-water, night diving and/or rescue diver. All these additional training steps can be accomplished over the months prior to the Underwater Photo Safari.

EQUIPMENT LEVEL

This activity involves confirming that you have all the equipment for the trip and that it still works. The first question deals with the amount of personal equipment you would like to carry with you on the trip. The camera gear is simple: whatever you need to have a successful Underwater Photo Safari. Much of this would be put in your "carry-on luggage" as it is expensive and you do not want it tossed around. The choice between high end photography equipment, such as single lens reflex cameras with strobes, versus point and shoot cameras leads to extensive equipment choices. In addition to purchasing the photography equipment, the question of weight and compactness rears its ugly head. The difference between easy carry vs. the complex photography option is discussed in the chapter on photography.

Small Wall Crab
Pentax Optio S5i,
5 megPix
Flash: auto
Settings: auto
Distance: macro

As to SCUBA gear, you definitely need mask (2), fins, snorkel, dive computer, skins/wetsuit, booties, gloves, BC, octopus, and backups. If you need to travel light, you can usually rent the heavy items such as BC or regulator. The question becomes one of how much should you pack vs. rent during a long trip. (Must let them know what you need to rent prior to showing up) One key item is batteries... buy early, charge up often, recheck prior to trip, and charge again. We simplify the problem of equipment by standardizing on AA's with battery charger. For each different size of battery you use, you will need a separate charger. Unfortunately, most digital cameras use company specific batteries; require unique spares and specific changes. One recommended approach is for your SCUBA team to standardize on photo equipment and batteries. This enables sharing of backups and reduces equipment load.

One key item at each stage of planning is packing for the airline and weight control. Plan to weigh your bags when you pack to make sure you will be within weight limits. It is too late when you are at the airport counter. As most of the Underwater Photo Safaris are going to remote destinations in the sun, additional items must be purchased and packed to include sunscreen, hat, sunglasses and bug spray.

One item that must be discussed prior to departure is the need for insurance. There are three categories of insurance you should think about. The *first* is medical. You should check with your service on how to be covered on a trip to exotic locations and which shots you should have. The *second* is dive insurance. This is usually purchased through DAN (Divers Alert Network) because of their excellent reach around the world with specific knowledge in SCUBA injury, recovery, and location of nearest decompression chambers. The *third* type of coverage is trip insurance. This is optional and recommended if you would have trouble accepting the loss of airline ticket, hotel deposits or boat down payments. There are over 100 trip insurance companies listed at Http:..insuremytrip.com. In addition, many of your homeowner policies may cover your dive gear through special riders. Our recommendation is to evaluate your insurance needs well before departure. We usually combine options by ensuring personal medical insurance covers our location and ensure coverage for diving through DAN. We do not buy camera insurance, however many do.

CHECKLIST FOR MID-RANGE PLANNING

Medium-Term Actions	Completed
M arrange care for animals/pets/lawn/flowers	_____
M boat, will diving be from small tenders	_____
M boat, will there be a camera table and rinse tank	_____
M boat, will there be a changing room and bathroom (head)	_____
M charge rechargeable batteries prior to trip; let sit for 20 days; test and check for batteries that have discharged; indicates a week battery; toss them out.	_____
M check all O-rings on lights and cameras	_____
M check your electrical devices to see if they are compatible with the electricity in the area you are going or transiting	_____
M customs and import restrictions, understand what they are and be ready to comply	_____
M dive trip planning parties; get together and check individual progress. This will provide support and motivation for getting things done.	_____
M diving conditions, will we be doing shore diving, beach or boat	_____
M diving conditions, read the reviews in magazines and on line news groups	_____
M diving conditions, what is the water temperature, do I need a wet suit, review thickness of hood, gloves and wet suit	_____
M diving conditions, will be doing shallow, wall, or wreck diving	_____
M diving conditions, will the current be still or strong drift diving	_____
M diving conditions, will the seas be rough open water or calm, sheltered diving	_____
M diving equipment rentals, does the dive shop rent equipment, do you need to reserve it	_____
M diving level, what skill level is required, beginner, intermediate, experienced, or professional	_____
M diving, are there training courses I can take	_____

M diving, are there training courses I need _____

M electrical voltage and wall plug design for each county and _____
ship you will visit or be on; it may change in the same
country, find out what they are and read the power supply on
your equipment; will it work; do I need a plug adaptor

M entertainment in the local area, tours, shopping, museums, _____
parks, music, food, farming, golf, site seeing; see the local area

M get Divers Alert Network (DAN) SCUBA diving insurance _____

M get necessary shots/vaccinations/prescriptions (malaria, _____
tetanus, Hep A&B, polio . . .)

M have regulator serviced _____

M insurance, do get overseas medical, scuba diving and _____
medical evacuation insurance

M insurance, should I get lost luggage or canceled trip
Insurance _____

M local area, maps, get maps of where you are going; will _____
greatly improve your enjoyment knowing where you are
going and have been.

M local history and culture, buy books and read about them. _____
You will enjoy a lot more of what you see on the trip

M local reputation of tour organization/hotel/resort/dive outfits _____
check on line and in magazines

M Luggage and weight restrictions, understand what they are _____
so you won't be caught with overweight issues

M luggage size restrictions, if your bag is too big, you will have _____
to check it. Many small airlines (island hoppers) have almost
no overhead storage.

M make copy of medical prescriptions (take with you) _____

M make copy of optical prescription (take with you) _____

M make list of contact phone numbers you may need to call _____
(family, friends, work to tell them you may be late)

M reconfirm all hotel reservations _____

M reconfirm all resort reservations _____

M reconfirm dive operation arrangements _____

M safety, what are the local diving safety requirements, _____
do you need special equipment

NOTES: _____

_____

_____

_____

CHAPTER 4:   NEAR TERM PREPARATION

This chapter covers the essential elements of getting ready for the trip. This would include the short-term activities such as:

- Ensure you have all items on the checklist
- Pack three-days early
- Check on airline reservations and seats

- Arrange transportation to/from airport
- Recharge all batteries
- Checkout images on storage media

NEAR TERM PREPARATION

One step that we found very effective is to completely pack three-days prior to take off. Two things happen: (1) You go through the checklist and ensure you have all your clothes and equipment ready for travel, and (2) you weigh the bags to make sure you are within your airline's limits. However, one caution, you must put everything in the bag, such as charged batteries or diving skins.

Memorable Event   *Forgot Something*

Another nice benefit of being at the boat departure location two days early is that you can review/inventory all your belongings and identify any item left behind. In Pete's case for Grenada, his SCUBA skins were still hanging where he had placed them to dry. We searched around the island for a XXX sized skin and failed to fill the void on the checklist. Luckily, Dennis brought two skins and one was his size. It is rewarding to bring spare parts that are actually used.   USE your Checklist!

A recommendation is to NOT plan to sneak anything into the bag at the last minute as it may "bust" 50 lbs and/or you may forget it.   Each person develops their own style of accomplishing the objective of accounting for all items; however, one approach that works is to place all items in a pile three or four days prior to the trip and keep adding to the pile as the checklist is reviewed. This allows you to double check your list as things go from your piles to your luggage.

Small Blue Spong
Pentax Optio S5i, 5 megPix
Flash: auto
Settings: auto
Distance: macro

The next thing you need to do is check airline reservations to ensure no flight times have been changed and your seats are still acceptable. An email to your hotel requesting late (or early) check-in will confirm they still have you on their books. After that, a thorough battery check is recommended as some go bad on the shelf and should be charged to make sure they still hold it. A check of your storage media would be worthwhile to confirm you have your camera cards and that they are empty of valuable family pictures you do not want to write over.

DAY OF TRAVEL

Remember, international travel requires patience. Early arrival at the airport helps ensure your bags are checked onto the correct flights while you have time to go through security and have a Starbucks – after all it is a vacation. Plenty of reading material could include camera or SCUBA computer operations manuals as well as novels.

LAND STAY PRIOR TO LIVE ABOARD

In a previous trip to the Galapagos, we spent four days in Quito, Ecuador, prior to boarding the boat. On this trip to Grenada we spent two days at the True Blue Bay Resort prior to boarding the boat. During the spare time it is important to call home and read your operations manuals. The plan for a live aboard Underwater Photo Safari should include from one to four days at your land destination prior to loading onto the dive boat. This allows your team to gather and also:

- Allows your body to recover from flights across time zones
- Enables your luggage to catch up with you
- Provides a delightful time to see the local culture and historic sites
- Provides an opportunity to conduct shore diving or local boat diving
- Allows you to replace parts or supplies you have forgotten
- Allows you to call the dive operator and confirm arrangements
- Confirms the date, location, and time of pickup for the live aboard

---

Memorable Event   *Classic Case of Flexibility*
– PNG to Bahamas

Our dive group had committed to go to Papua New Guinea (PNG) in June 2003. Each of us had made reservations, arranged commitments from work, and packed our bags. A massive thunderstorm came into the east coast causing flights to be cancelled. Some were not able to recover on their travel itinerary heading for the Pacific. The decision had to be made on the spot.... should two of four go as planned and dive as half of the team [Feedback from airlines was there were to be no seats available for ten days]; or, should they be flexible and re-plan on the go for some unknown alternative as a full dive team. After many cell phone calls, the decision was to redirect our trip to the Bahamas – a different hemisphere of the Earth, a different type of diving and a different setup of hotels, airfares and boat charges. With amazing teamwork and coordination/cooperation from Peter Hughes' dive planning, the team changed boats while on the move. Luckily, the expenses for the change were minimum as the airlines allowed us to rebook as it was weather related. Peter Hughes transferred the money from PNG to their Bahamas boat. Multiple nights down payment of hotel reservations became the only expenses of the change. In addition, the Caribbean trip added one more diver from our group who could commit to the shorter trip. Can you imagine starting out toward PNG and ending up in Georgetown Bahamas?

CHECKLIST FOR NEAR TERM PLANNING

Short-Term Actions	**Completed**
S alcohol, tobacco, foods, what products can you take into or out of the places you will visit	_____
S call credit card companies, tell them you are going overseas so they may adjust your spending profile	_____
S check dive computer battery/change if you have doubt	_____
S diving gas, does the resort have NITROX	_____
S fishing restrictions, what can you do in the vacation area, pole fishing, spear fishing or none	
S food and organic products, what can you take into or out of the places you will visit	_____
S food, tell the resorts if you have any special food or dietary needs	_____
S get necessary pills (prescriptions, over the counter, malaria, vitamins, . .)	_____
S internet, is there internet in your vacation area at the hotel/resort/café so you may send emails to your friends at work and tell them how much fun you are having on vacation	_____
S label everything; keeps it from getting mixed up	_____
S lay out all dive equipment from head to foot to make certain you have it all prior to packing	_____
S lay out all camera equipment in its proper place to make certain you have it all; also it is good to hook it all up and check it out.	_____
S Luggage, mark luggage with colored tape or string; makes it easier to find in the airport and hotel	_____
S luggage, put two name tags on each piece, they tend to get ripped off	_____
S make copies of your Cert-cards, passport, visas and other papers (swap with travel buddy)	_____

S   money in local area; what kind do they use, how do you   _____
convert, do they have ATMs, WHERE can you do it, do they
take credit cards

S   pack everything in plastic bags, keeps it dry and easy to sort   _____

S   pets, arrange for someone to take care of them or take them   _____
to a pet boarding facility

S   phone numbers and emails where you will be, make a list   _____
and give to your family and friends at home so they can
contact you

S   phone numbers and emails of the resorts and tour   _____
companies you are going to visit so you can take on trip

S   phone numbers and emails, make list of the folks at home   _____
so you can contact them

S   phone service in your vacation area, is there service   _____
(in some remote areas, there is NO phone service)

S   phone service, will you cell phone work in the vacation area   _____

S   plants, arrange for someone to take care of your plants   _____

S   plants, what can you take into or out of the places you visit   _____

S   reconfirm all airline reservations and seat assignments   _____

S   refill medical prescriptions (we cannot stress this enough)   _____

S   reconfirm all hotel reservations   _____

S   reconfirm all resort reservations   _____

S   reconfirm dive operation arrangements   _____

S   smoking restrictions, what are the guidelines for the hotels,   _____
resorts, and dive boats you will visiting/using/staying with

S   smoking restrictions, will you be traveling with smokers or   _____
non-smokers - be considerate

S   smoking, what tobacco can you take into or out of the places   _____
you will visit

S   sharpen all knifes and lightly coat with oil   _____

S   State Department, check their web site for current   _____
information on the local political situation

S   State Department, get location and contact information of _____
    the local US Embassy services

S   State Department, register your overseas trip with State _____
    Department, important for remote and unstable political areas

S   stop home snail mail, newspapers and deliveries _____

S   tell neighbors you are going, AGAIN, give them your contact _____
    info, get/veryfy their contact info

S   tipping expectations, research what is expected, what is too _____
    much, what is the norm, how do you tip, what currency do
    you use, can you use credit cards

S   write down CC numbers and international phone numbers _____
    to call CC companies

S   weigh luggage; repack or toss out stuff if bags are too heavy _____

S   take copies of the wavers you sent in advance and _____
    give to dive company   (this will save you from filling them
    out again, forms tend to get lost)

S   go to your luggage pile and toss out 10 pounds, you _____
    packed too much!!!

S   diver certification cards; DO YOU HAVE THEM!! _____

S   get short haircut _____

Action Things: Do NOT take on the trip   Completed

-illegal drugs with you; foreign laws are very tough and the _____
    jails are not nice

-scuba tanks, they are very heavy and provided by most scuba _____
    operations as part of your dive charter

-weights, they are very heavy and provided by most scuba _____
    operations as part of your dive charter

-heavy books, take paperbacks and swap books with others _____
    on the trip; use the local take one, leave one library

-food, most items are prohibited and will be seized at customs
       when entering a country, buy local; remember, you are   _____
       on an adventure
-too many cloths; use items that can be cleaned in your room   _____
       on the trip or use hotel laundry
-large containers of liquids; they are heavy, use travel sizes or   _____
       buy local
-you may want to rent heavy regulators or BCs from your dive   _____
       operation; saves a LOT of luggage weight.

NOTES: _____

_____

_____

_____

CHAPTER 5: CONCURRENT ACTIVITIES AND PLANNING

This chapter approaches the real fun of meeting new people, establishing your base of operations for cameras and computers, and settling into your room. This chapter breaks out the characteristics and strengths/shortfalls of live aboard and land resort based vacations. The reason for this breakout is that there are significant differences in the adventures when comparing the live aboard or land resort based Underwater Photo Safari. Major differences are:

- Flexibility of entertainment such as golf vs. diving or shopping vs. sunning (land based strength).
- Increased choices in the social arena such as dining, dating or nightlife (land based strengths).
- Less complexity to diving with everything stored onboard (live aboard strength).
- Intense and focused diving for the full week (live aboard strength).

Feather Duster Tube Worm
Pentax Optio S5i,
5 megPix
Flash: auto
Settings: Auto

This chapter also explains the processes upon which you exist for the full week of vacation. The routine for diving, eating, and sleeping can be fun to get wrapped around. There are many similarities, and many variables, when comparing live aboard and land based Underwater Photo Safaris. Many of the pleasant surprises center around non-diving experiences such as eating, sleeping, excursions, and exercise. At the end of the chapter is "A Travelers Ten Commandments" that deals with excellent rules to live by when traveling internationally. In addition to the many differences, there are many common activities which include:

- Meet the diving crew
- Investigate the facilities
- Ensure all bags made it
- Photo equipment facilities
- Room arrangements -- unpack and put away clothes

LIVE ABOARD UNDERWATER PHOTO SAFARI

This section of the book breaks out the activities of a live aboard with subsections on (a) first day at vacation location, (b) first day aboard, and (c) living on the boat.

First Day at Vacation Location: The first day on vacation usually starts at the hotel you have booked as a time lag for you and your group. The hotel can usually set you up for late checkout, if the loading of the boat is in the afternoon; or, you could sit in the bar and store your bags with the concierge. This is a good time to get to know the people who are going to be on the boat with you for a week or to check out the instruction manual for that new piece of equipment. In Pete's case, the question was how to set up the new dive computer for NITROX. In addition, photo recording the hotel, first days of travel and the boat with your above water camera can set up the first few images of your final trip DVD.

First Day on the Boat: Usually, you are met by an attentive crew [captain, dive masters/instructors, hostess, and cooks] in the salon and welcomed with either lunch or dinner. This is a good time to have fun with your dive buddies by selecting a few tables that are close together and relax. At the beginning of the trip, it is always better to enjoy those you traveled with [after all, you traveled half way around the world with them because they are your friends]. Natural phenomena will occur during the week that will find you moving around the tables and getting to know the others on the boat. This is a major portion of the enjoyment gained from being on a live aboard trip. Boat members come from the most wonderful places and each have multiple stories of diving around the world. The initial cocktail party is a great place to start the discussions relative to future locations you may want to visit. Many come with photos and everyone definitely comes with stories of the best of this and the best of that even if it's their first trip. How they got there and why is always fascinating.

The bags and gear are taken to the boat and the crew usually places your dive gear up on deck and your personal stuff in your room. This makes it much easier to understand the layout of the boat before you have any "test" like how to get to your room. There is a quick welcome and general discussion about the boat and safety items. Soon after you become comfortable on the boat, and after the lunch or dinner, you need to unload your bags inside your room. The rooms are definitely not big, so the storage of all your stuff in the closets and drawers is the only answer if you are to have a happy bunkmate. The bags then go in closets or are stored by the crew. Now remember, especially for those of us who are not necessarily neat-freaks, the rooms are extremely small and organization and storage is important. Your roommate will appreciate you being somewhat neat; or, at least keep your mess on your bunk. One secret that experienced Underwater Photo Safari divers learn is the necessity of drying your bathing suits outside in the winds off the sea. This is accomplished by attaching a carabineer to any structure on deck with the bathing suit tied on. When ready for the next dive, you just switch suits, wet for dry without cluttering up the small bathroom in the cabin. Remember to keep out reading material. As you lounge around the boat between dives or motor to the next dive site the pleasure of just "vegging out" can be wonderful.

Memorable Events   Baggage Backup

During a trip to the Bahamas, one day was planned as spare time to account for luggage and people delivery to the kickoff point. One of the travel partners showed up with only his hand-carry luggage and was promised that the luggage would definitely get there prior to the boat leaving. The luggage was lost on a flight that was cancelled in Miami and then did not make the flight the following day. OOPS… He was on the boat with one change of clothing, two bathing suits and his camera equipment because he violated the rule to have sufficient days for luggage to catch up. The good news was that we had a large contingent of travel companions who had enough backup equipment to cover his needs. The boat supplied the regulator and the BC while we had a spare mask, snorkel, fins, skins, dive lights, batteries, desiccant, and even spare underwater camera. It is good to have friends with plenty of backup equipment.

In parallel with settling in to the boat surroundings is the task of setting up your gear. You can proceed to load your dive gear into a chosen location on the dive deck and ensure that you have all the parts you need. One of the secrets is to claim a good corner for you and your buddy (or buddies) where you can all get geared up together and gear down with help. This is the best location to do a safety check of each other's gear. In our group, one consistently bungee cords himself to the boat. Getting in and out of wetsuits usually takes a friendly tug here and there. After all, this is a pleasure trip, not a dive card test activity. The gear layout usually stays the same for the full week with tanks being refilled and the fins and masks being located below the bench. On the Grenada boat, the whole operation centered around tenders so all of your gear was placed upon each tender initially set up by each individual. We fixed our equipment up within an hour of being on the boat and had everything loaded onto our bc's so the parts would not be lost as we fell into the water.

Underwater cameras are always special when on a SCUBA boat. Peter Hughes' boats usually have a large table in a central area dive deck. This allows you to assemble the strobe arms and place all the key elements of the apparatus together. Being at an outside temperature eliminates the "fogging" problems which occur after transitioning cameras from the air conditioning area to the humid outside location. Prior to the dive, you just need to check on batteries, ensure you have disciscent, properly close up the package, do a functional test, and hand the camera to a crew member to then give it to you in the water.

Black Coral Silhouette
Pentax Optio S5i, 5 megPix
Flash: off
Settings: auto
Distance: infinity

The fun of setting up the camera and making sure that it is safe to enter the water is one of the most enjoyable parts of an Underwater Photo Safari. Early placement of your camera and apparatus on the camera table works as a "claim" in most cases which enables you to leave your equipment in place while you are elsewhere. The travel boxes and spare parts go below the table on nice storage shelves so the whole photography equipment package is in one location. This enables easy access to items necessary to conduct photo operations such as: reading glasses holder, mask clear liquid, ear cleanser, memory cards, tools, desiccant, spare batteries, and of course, backup equipment. Early in your trip (I like to do it on the first day) the camera assembly consumes some time and ensures that you are ready for the first dive. On the trip to Grenada, the fact that we had not been diving for a year, the layout was strange, and we were diving on tenders, drove us to not dive with cameras on the first dive. The old trick of remembering how to have buoyancy control, regain your comfort in the water and learn how to work in and out of the tender led us to the conclusion that the use of a camera on the first day was just one step too many. On the first day, you want to prep the camera setup so that it is ready when you are ready to take pictures.

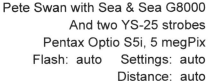

Pete Swan with Sea & Sea G8000
And two YS-25 strobes
Pentax Optio S5i, 5 megPix
Flash: auto   Settings: auto
Distance: auto

Memorable Event   *Camera Loss*

One of the fears for all Underwater Photo Safari participants is that you will get on the boat, move away from supply stores, and lose the camera on the first dive. Yep! This exact fear happened to Pete in the Galapagos. He traveled 5,000 miles to the islands, set up the camera anticipating recording the unique marine life in this phenomenal national marine park, and then on the first dive his camera leaked at 50'. By the time he surfaced, the seawater had combined with the battery acid to "toast" his underwater camera. Ouch – his whole trip was over after one dive! Hurray for buddies – they had backup cameras so he could have a successful Underwater Photo Safari after all.

LIVING ON THE BOAT

The beauty of choosing a live aboard is that once you have shucked bags from the hotel to the dock, the stress is over. Once your gear is set up, it stays that way until you pack (different than a day boat approach). For one week, the key elements of the trip are simple; go to bed, get up, breakfast, dive, snack, dive, lunch, dive, snack, dive, dinner, and drinks (or night dive and then drinks). The pattern is established on the first day; and then, efforts to maintain a pattern are minimal. The choice is yours as to how many dives, when to dive and how to play while on the boat. A key to enjoying this activity is to recognize that you will be sharing a small room on a large boat with a buddy. This demands some compromises such as putting all your stuff in drawers or hang-ups as soon as possible. The shower is usually so small that we have developed a technique: soap the sides of the shower and then rotate around for the soap. Most of the time on the boat is spent with others in the common lounge area. This is truly fun as you meet and enjoy people from many locations and backgrounds. The day-to-day activities are repetitive; but, the dives are all different and the fish vary significantly from dive site to dive site. If you choose not do all five dives per day (usually max offered with down time measured by your dive computer in the conservative mode), you are sure to miss the greatest seahorse stampede or the wildest sea lion game of tag. One wonders where the divers get these great "fish tales" because they never happen when you are down there. The variety of the sea and the constant motion will ensure that each dive is unique and an experience to remember.

The meals on a live aboard are usually first rate because the Captain does not want a mutiny. Can you imagine a boat with 20 divers and 10 crew that has modest food? Not quite! The key to this type of trip is that you are on the ocean and the fruit of the sea ends up on your table. Lobster thermidor was provided on Wednesday night as the locals had picked them out of the sea around 2 pm and sold them to us from a little dingy in time for dinner. Fruit and vegetables were always there with the selection of fish, pork, chicken and beef. Each meal was more than the divers needed; but, each of us enjoyed the food with the excuse that we earned it expending calories for heat and exercise.

One of the events you should not miss while on a live aboard is the never-ending beauty of the sunrises and sunsets. If one plans well, the view from the upper deck is spectacular with the often-stated claim of... "Of course I saw the green flash." [a rare natural phenomenon that occurs as the rays of the sun go through more and more atmosphere – literally bending over the horizon] After thousands of sunsets over the ocean, I still have not seen the green flash with its instantaneous surprise after the sun disappears. However, the pictures of the sunset/sunrise with clouds over the ocean or islands make for memories that are with you forever.

LAND BASED UNDERWATER PHOTO SAFARI

This section of the chapter discusses the land based Underwater Photo Safari. This is broken down into (a) first day at the resort, and (b) day by day activities.

First Day at Resort: The first day at your resort is always a treat after the trip planning and effort to get there. One recommendation is that you should not "run-through" your check-in process. That is the best time to ask questions and try to understand the "lay-of-the-land." The daily routine needs to be understood, especially the meal service times, happy hour locations, sports schedules, excursion options, and Underwater Photo Safari opportunities. After the full group has checked in, a planning gathering should be conducted to feel out the best times and days to take advantage of the various choices. In our group, we have some who want to dive five times a day, some who want to shop, some who really want to lay-back, and those who want to do it all. Once again – centralized planning and individual execution enables each to maximize the enjoyment of the trip. Another task early in the week is to provision the room with items necessary to survive a week in paradise. This would include soft drinks of choice, type of alcohol, snacks and maybe even breakfasts for the week.

Transportation at the resorts comes in many flavors and depends upon the needs of the group. If the location is an all-in-one type, maybe there is no need for your own car/van; however, if the group wants to go to off-site dinners, make shore dives or wants to explore as a small team – rental cars or taxis need to be arranged.

One of the first items to accomplish once you have settled into your room is to set up the SCUBA equipment and prepare for the first dive. This ranges from pre-positioning the equipment on a large boat, leaving it in lockers near the pier, or dedicating a portion of the room to equipment. Often our team has come into one of our rooms and not been able to see any flat surface. Camera equipment, especially, occupies specific areas for their "care and feeding." Of course the shower room is over used rinsing everything. Early preparation ensures that you put everything together and check out your ability to turn it on or assemble it. Oops – I forgot something so I need to see if the local shop has it or I have to go into my backup equipment stack. This is also a good time to check out the dive shop and show them your diver certifications.

Memorable Event   *Wreck Rental*

   Even though Pete rented through his global service, the car at the airport would not support a group of seven with extra SCUBA bags. After negotiations, the van that was offered was unique and especially appreciated for the roomy arrangements. However, the holes in the floorboard at the drivers peddles enabled the road surface to be seen. In addition, when he walked away from the car with the keys, it often continued to run. What adventures we have on the road!

Day by Day Activities at the Land Based Resort: One of the planning challenges for dive resorts is to schedule the important excursions around the local area against potential dive activities. Usually there are two-dive boats in the morning and afternoon so vast choices exist. Of course you would want to ask the dive shop for the dive locations and relative merits of each so you can decrease repeat dive locations and ensure you are there when the team discovers that one memorable event. The preliminary schedule of what to do and when to do it usually starts at the dive shop when investigating locations. The choices are often remarkable, such as the one Pete took to wander the jungles of Papua New Guinea in search of WW II airplanes instead of a morning boat dive. The pictures were amazing from the trip, of course. During the week at the resort there will be many events that should not be missed. Introduction to the local culture and historic sites is always worthwhile. There may be movies, lectures or dances that should not be missed. Our group usually ensures communications through meetings at meals. This enables us to gather and talk about adventures experienced and plan for the next few days: when to SCUBA, when to go to town, and when to relax. Ensure you bring the necessary tools to really relax – books, DVDs and player, golf clubs, tennis racquets, or just sun glasses and sun screen.

The Peter Hughes Dive operators have consolidated the "rules of the road" for Underwater Photo Safaris. This list of common sense seemed very "real" to us after experiencing the good and bad of SCUBA adventures. As such, we have copied the list from the Peter Hughes' website, to recognize the desires of the boat operators to have a glorious experience for all. As you prepare for your journey to a foreign land, faithful observance of the "Travelers Ten Commandments" can be very rewarding:

A Travelers Ten Commandments[3]

I. Thou shalt not expect to find things as thou hast left them at home, for thou hast left thy home to find things different.
II. Thou shalt not take anything too seriously, for a carefree mind is the beginning of a vacation.
III. Thou shalt not let the other tourist get on thy nerves, for thou art paying good money to have a good time.
IV. Thou shalt know where thy passport is at all times, for a person without a passport is a person without a country.
V. Thou shalt always remember that thou art a representative of thy country at all times.
VI. Blessed is the person who can say "thank you" in any language, that and a smile shall double the value of any tip thou mayst give.
VII. Thou shalt not worry, for the person who worries hath no pleasure, and few things are ever fatal.
VIII. Thou shalt not judge the people of a country by one person whith whom thou hast had trouble.

---

[3] Peter Hughes website, www.peterhughes.com, Dec 2007.

IX. Thou shalt when in Rome do as the Romans do, and if in difficulty, thou shalt use Common Sense – a Friendly smile and kind disposition.

X. Thou shalt remember thou art a guest in every land, and who treateth its host with respect shall be treated as an honored guest.

CHECKLIST FOR DAY OF TRAVEL

Action Things to do ON the trip	Completed
-call your dive tour company and let them know you have arrived in the vacation area and will be at the appropriate location for pick up as scheduled.	_____
-buy things for your trip book; maps, photos & postcards	_____
-get list of your dive sites	_____
-get list of the passengers on your dive boat, resort and hotels	_____
-keep activity list and opinions for reference at the end of the cruse/stay when you write the performance critique/ feedback for the boat/hotel, good feedback is also needed	_____
-make list of things you need for your next trip	_____
-notify your home family/neighbors of your travel & progress of your trip; they want to know you are ok	
-purchases, make list of what you buy so you can put on customs list when you reenter the US (see US Customs and Boarder Protection CBP Publicaion No. 0000-00512)	_____
-start lessons learned list	_____

NOTES: _____

_____

_____

_____

CHAPTER 6:   PREPARING FOR PHOTOGRAPHIC ACTIVITIES

The skill of taking pictures above and below water can always be improved. This continuous improvement process is a lifetime effort with Underwater Photo Safaris a significant step towards, at least, below water improvement.

- Taking the pictures: The choice of cameras, approach to the underwater environment, and the skill of the photographer leads to a few spectacular images among many attempts.
- Working with the pictures: There are many ways to approach the manipulation of photos. Your choice of computer drives you toward either iPhoto or Photo Elements software.
- Storing the pictures: Keeping track of photos and memorable events on the adventure requires some time and energy to pull it all together.
- Sharing the pictures: Many in the group and others on the boat have various views of similar dives; but, frequently, they are worthy images and should be shared. [Bring blank DVDs]

Camera Table, Sea Dancer
Turks & Caicos June 2002
Nikon CoolPix 5000
Flash: off   Settings: auto
Distance: normal

PHOTOGRAPHY APPROACH

The beauty of diving with cameras is that the underwater scenic variety you observe, you *really* observe. The concentration necessary for a photographer to accomplish a goal is great. The underwater photographer is usually focused upon pre-determined objectives such as MACRO imaging of small things such as shrimp, wide angle shots of large movers such as whale sharks, or precise, color enhanced, non-movers such as sea fans. The diver who is a photographer also has two sets of equipment (SCUBA & photo) that they must set up and then carry with them to and from a dive site. These extra complexities become special capabilities after they fall into the water and the underwater world wakes up. A good example of this is the simple fact that most divers never notice the "tails" of all the fish they see; whereas, the Underwater Photo Safari participate ends up with one heck of a lot of tails in their photography. This surprise occurs because of the time lag of the point and shoot cameras between pushing the button, the automatic focusing, and the actual "snap" of the picture. We underwater photographers work very hard to pose our subjects, but they do not always cooperate very well. Hence: lots of tails in our pictures. The good news is that digital photography has taken over and all it takes is a push of the delete button and the tails are gone and only good pictures are left to enjoy. We have often thought of publishing a book of "sea tails." The shutter delay can virtually be eliminated by switching to a single lens reflex camera in a large housing. [Most of the photos in this book were taken with small cameras.]

If one were to divide up Underwater Photo Safari camera types, one would choose between "point and shoot," high end single lens reflex cameras, or video capabilities. Each has its own strengths and weaknesses, while always a joy to participate in something extra while underwater. The preparation for each type varies, but each requires the care and feeding of the devices from camera to flash units to computer support. Then there is the differentiation due to types of underwater subjects. Most of us have predetermined targets prior to entering the water. Some of these include the non-movers such as corals, sponges, fans or rock formations. Another category we actively pursue is the "small stuff" with macro lens. One of the most satisfying dives we ever made was one focusing on clownfish inside sea anemones. The third category is usually the big movers such as groupers, turtles (a favorite), sharks, and seals; with the ultimate being the whales and whale sharks. Each of these categories requires pre-dive setup of the cameras. If you have a wide-angle lens for the big stuff, you will have trouble doing macro and vice versa. In addition, the flash vs. strobe vs. natural light leads to multiple equipment set-ups. One thought that continues to "bug-you" is the realization that there are the dive photographers who HAVE flooded their cameras and there are dive photographers who WILL flood their cameras. There are no other type of Underwater Photo Safari photographers!

Our process for preparing for the variety of three types of underwater targets requires multiple steps. Some underwater photo steps are:

- Get Ready Prior to Trip
- Practice General Techniques
- Approach to be Ready (charge batteries, etc.)
- Have lots of backup – team coordination for backups works well
- Don't cry when things break or flood as it is an opportunity to update your camera equipment when you get home

With underwater photography, there are natural issues for which you try to compensate. The loss of color as you go down in depth is a real photographic issue that must be enhanced during the processing of the image. The first step, obviously, is to ensure that your flash is on for all shots. Another factor is that you need to be close enough to the subject for the flash to be effective. The only way to see color beyond 15 feet deep is through an effective flash or strobe light. The loss of color really restricts the "beauty" of the photo unless you are very effective in the flash direction, timing and strength. As you progress into this hobby, you will notice that serious amateurs are carrying many more bags than you to handle the extra strobes and larger underwater cases. The drive for faster shutter speeds [get away from just tails] and more strobe lights ends up with longer strobe arms and heavier equipment. The combination is designed to defeat the basic fact that depth of water filters out the color from the sunlight. While you are underwater, you will be amazed at the beauty and diversity of the life. However, when you surface and show the pictures from the strobes and the flashes the colors amaze you. Was that fish really that yellow? Was that seahorse really dark green vs. black? An amazing realization occurs when you are investigating the shots and revel in the "lucky" images that show up on the computer.

PREPARATION FOR UNDERWATER PHOTOGRAPHY

In addition to the preparation for an Underwater Photo Safari trip, the preparation for the photography is fun and challenging. Getting ready prior to the trip ensures that the photographic part of the trip is as successful as the vacation part. There are many aspects of preparation that must be accomplished prior to departure. The choice of type of photographic equipment is definitely a large one with many variables. Early purchase ensures "having all the parts." In addition, checkout of the equipment is necessary to make sure the parts fit together as advertised. Both above water practice and below water practice (pool work helps avoid salt water leaks) helps you to understand the make-up of the equipment. Practice is necessary to ensure that you know how to image in the MACRO world as well as automatic settings. Selection of the correct computer and software varies with the type of camera and type of computer (MAC vs. PC). Practice taking images, downloading them to the chosen computer and manipulating the images is critical prior to the big trip. In addition, the weight of all these items must be accounted for prior to getting onto an airplane. Once you have reached your destination, the preparation does not stop. Being prepared to have your camera ready for the first dive takes planning and, usually, assembly of your equipment. After you have set up your camera gear, frequent re-charging of the batteries is required.

PHOTOGRAPHY CHOICES PRIOR TO THE TRIP

Choosing the Camera: Half of the fun of an Underwater Photo Safari is handling the pictures once they are taken and the other half is choosing the camera gear. If you are a gear geek, you will really love this hobby with complex equipment sets. What type of camera is right for you? Prior to answering that question you must set some guidelines such as: How much money are you willing to spend? How sophisticated do you need? And, how much do you want to carry?

I am not talking about how many megapixels you need because all current digital cameras have sufficient megapixels. The hard question on an extensive Underwater Photo Safari is how much do you want to carry. The next image shows the difference is size for cameras that have similar megapixal counts. The camera on the left, a Pentax Optio S5i with its Pentax UW housing was used to take almost all the UW photos in this book, has 5 megapixals. The camera on the right is a Nikon D70 with 6 megapixals and a large complex housing and strobes. The Pentax is very easy to carry on a trip. It is so small it can actually fit into the Altoids can next to it. However, the Pentax has a very small flash, so you must get very close to your subject while it takes 15 seconds or so for the camera to recharge between photos. This may drive many people nuts when confronted with "priceless" opportunities underwater which may require many photos in rapid session. If you want to take photos as fast as you can push the button, the Nikon D70 on the right will do that. With the strobes set on half power so they recharge in less that one second, you can take photos once a second for many seconds. The next difference is auto focus time. The Pentax can take 2 seconds or so to focus while the Nikon will focus in less than a second. This is important if you are taking pictures of fish.

Camera Choices,
Left to right; Pentax O-WP2 underwater case, for the Pentax Optio S5i, Altoids can, Nikon D70 with 10mm f/2.8 lens, Subal under-water housing for the D70 with two Sea and Sea YS-120 strobes.

We could write a whole book about the technical data of camera choices, and many have. Suffice it to say, cameras today are much better than when we were beginner photographers. Our objective is to advance our photography skills. One photo skill recommendation is to take a photo course at one of your local community colleges or other educational facilities to ensure you will be up to speed on the technical stuff. Do NOT wait to learn on the Underwater Photo Safari. The next decision is "how much do you want to carry?" There are many choices in how to carry your camera to include; soft backpacks, hard shell cases, plastic bags, foam bags, and just loose in your carry-on. The camera cases shown are very different. The Pelican case is small enough that it can be carried onboard almost any plane in the world. It will fit under a seat, it will go in an overhead bin and it can just sit on your lap on the small island hoppers. It will easily carry two small point and shoot cameras and their underwater cases. You can also toss in an external underwater strobe, the strobe arms, the sync cords and other necessary equipment. It can be locked and is strong enough so you can check it in the luggage. It will protect your equipment through all the bangs and thumps of the luggage animals. BUT, it says, "Look at ME, I am Expensive." Yes, Dennis has checked many cases like this and has never had a problem; but, his nerves are still tingling from wondering if it may be stolen. The case on the right is home made. He found an old suitcase in the trash and modified it. It is hard sided so it affords relatively good puncture protection. He filled the inside with large sheets of Styrofoam and cut holes in them to accept a large Nikon D70. The suitcase will carry the Subal housing, the large dome port you see in the previous photo, a smaller flat port not in the photo, two YS-120 strobes, the strobe arms, and sync cords, many batteries, the chargers, many flashlights, and lots of other little things. It is locked with a TSA luggage strap and has wheels for dragging around the airport. The grey stripe on the side is duct tape (remember the checklist), which provides a distinctive marking so Dennis can recognize the bag on the luggage carrousel. And the bag says "nothing but a cheap bag." When he drags it onto a dive boat, even the crew does not suspect it has photo gear and keep trying to take it to his cabin.

Camera Cases,
From left to right, Pelican 1500, Samsonite used suitcase from dump

The Grenada crew's jaws dropped open; and then, they began to laugh when he opened it up and took out $15,000USD worth of photo gear. He has used this case many times and it has never failed him. But, it is BIG.

So, what camera should you get? We recommend you purchase a <u>small point and shoot with the manufacture's UW housing</u>. You should be able to find a very nice starter camera for under a $1,000 USD. Sea and Sea, Canon and Olympus are very common choices and will serve you well. There are several other manufactures who also make excellent camera and housing combinations. Dennis uses a Pentax model which is not made anymore. He chose the Pentax because it was the smallest camera on the market at the time. He has used Nikons in Nikon UW housings and they work very well. If you don't want the manufacture's UW housing you can move up to a 2nd party housing. Ikelite makes excellent housings and has probably the best customer support in the word. They have been in business for years and fully guarantee everything they make. Dennis has had only a few problems with their equipment and they repaired it quickly without any hesitation. The Ikelite housing costs more than the manufacture's housings but are of better quality and can be repaired. They are exceptionally strong and are made of a very clear plastic; however, they will be slightly larger than the manufacture's housing. Small cameras are very easy to carry and to care for. Many people try to use them out of their flash range underwater resulting in everything looking green and washed out. Small cameras are really excellent at macro photography. The photos in this book, with the exception of four, were taken at a distance of a few inches. One standard rule is to get as close as you can, then get closer. Set the camera to macro mode and the flash on auto. Compose your photo and shoot. Take your time and shoot again. The sea water filters the colors out of the sunlight except for the blues and greens at the depth you will be SCUBA diving. You must use the camera flash to add a wide spectrum of light back into the photo so you can see the fantastic colors in the fish, coral and plant life.

The larger camera choice with external strobes, will light up macro and also very wide angle photos. However, the big camera is very difficult to carry and I do not recommend it for the person who is just starting out. Take your little point and shoot camera, put it on the boat camera table with the photo pros on the boat and act like you are just starting. You will be surprised at how many people will be willing to help you get started. The tough part will be sorting out those who really know what they are doing and those who are only one day ahead of you. Learn how your camera works prior to getting on the boat. Take a local photo class. They will explain all your camera functions and then make you take practice photos. When you have experimented with multiple approaches, they critique your photos and your technique in a constructive manner. Remember, you are not trying to be the best photographer in the class. You are only trying to improve yourself. You will then be sent out on another photo assignment and the process starts all over again. The limitation of these classes is that they are structured for land photography. This leads naturally to boarding a boat and applying your land skills to UW photography. There are a few good rules that you should add to the land skills you have developed: 1- get as close as you can, then get closer, 2- focus on the fish eyes, and 3- work macro first. If you follow these three simple rules, you will return home with photos you will be proud to show your friends.

Choosing the Computer and Software: As with your camera selection decision, there is no one answer here that works for all, but there are some guidelines.

    a. select a very light laptop, you will be carrying it a lot,
    b. buy LOTS of RAM and a large internal hard drive,
    c. get an external hard drive for backup, and
    d. get an inexpensive photo processing software package.

The group I travel with uses Macintosh computers. We argue about all aspects of Macintosh; but, mostly we use the free included photo processing software, iPhoto. We can then process our still photos into movies with iDVD, add a nice sound track and then burn it to DVD. After we return home we pass the DVDs out to our friends to show our Underwater Photo Safari. However, do not become focused upon Mac or PC in the selection process of computers. That is a never ending argument. There is more software and hardware in both camps than any of us will ever use. Your camera will produce a very, very large number of photos during your trip and you will not want to trash them immediately. This leads to the conclusion that you will need a lot of hard drive space to save them. The idea is to buy the largest internal hard drive you can because you will be surprised at how fast it fills up.

Your photo processing software will require a lot of RAM. Do not acquire less than 2GB of RAM. If you have an old laptop and plan to take it on an Underwater Photo Safari, give it a try first. You may find it is too slow to process photos. If so, you must decide -- stay with the slow processing or upgrade your laptop. A hard choice but we find ourselves upgrading our laptops every 4 to 5 years.

The choice of software to handle your pictures is up to the photographer. There are many excellent packages; and, camera manufacturers regularly send you free software along with the camera. The basic software packages we work with, and are common among the professionals and serious amateurs, are: Photoshop Elements 6 (as of this book) and Apple iPhoto. Each has strengths and weaknesses so we usually work with both of them. The iPhoto has tremendous advantages for the person who is just working with photos and wants to play with them and store them and improve their presentation. The ease of an Apple product is well known and the iPhoto program continues with this strength. Many professionals use the MAC system because of the ease of use and robustness of its program. However, Photoshop Elements does play on both Macs and PCs and many serious photographers who own Macs have both and switch back and forth between the two programs. Each of the programs has excellent strengths and each has its own weaknesses; however, both support photographers well. The choice normally breaks down to the common dominator of which type of computer do you already have? Once that is established, the selection is a natural. PC'ers go with Photoshop Elements and MAC'ers go with iPhoto or a combination of both.

Something you should have is a CD/DVD burner in your laptop. You will want to burn your photos to a data CD or DVD and pass them out to your friends on the boat, or better yet, burn photos from your new friends to a data CD/DVD so you can take them home. A CD/DVD is also the best way to backup your photos for the trip home. They are very light, cheap, and most laptops come with a build in CD/DVD burner that will work just fine.

Memorable Event	Slow Computers
Dennis was on the Peter Hughes Komodo Dancer out of Bali, Indonesia, in June 2007. There were several very good photographers on the boat but they all had very old laptops without a DC/DVD burner. On the last night, they decided to swap photos while on the boat versus going home and promise to send them to each other. Fortunately, he had brought along several blank DVDs and was able to load all the photos from all the people onto his laptop. He then burned a data DVD for each of them to take home. The job was made easier because Dennis had brought along a photo card reader for CF, SD, memory stick and MMC style cards and several 8GB thumb drives so people could transfer photos from their laptops. It took him into the early morning hours to get it all done; but, it was worth it. Several of them will be traveling from around the world to join us on the Peter Hughes Paradise Dancer in Manado, Indonesia in June 2008. This small gesture of kindness bonded the friendships made on the trip.	

Surface Interval: Once you have taken your pictures underwater, you must surface and stay up for a period of time to re-establish your nitrogen levels. During this interval, it is a natural to pull out the camera battery [remember --- recharge, recharge, recharge....] and the data disk. Downloading of the data onto the computer can be done in many ways, but we enjoy doing it after each dive for two reasons: 1 – we ensure that the photos we thought we took actually ended up on the computer [did not leave the disk out or hit the wrong switch on the camera or not have a charged battery --- oops we've done all three], and 2 – we learn more effectively when we remember where we took the picture, what settings we was trying, whether the flash worked and what the water conditions were. This rapid feedback makes the next dive more effective in that you have checked the camera setup and double-checked your technique. In addition, if there is a "killer image" you really want, such as a certain fish or cluster of coral, you can go back (if the boat has not moved). Some people like to wait until the end of the day to enter their data onto the computer and some do not bring their computer so they must store their photos on disks until they return home. Each method has strengths; but, we really enjoy the rapid feedback and the fun of playing with the photos immediately. Another thing to remember is that if you are on vacation, you do not have as many distractions, such as the realities of life. You have time to enjoy working on the photos, as it is part of the big adventure. Once you return home, the priority of refining your pictures goes down tremendously. Things like life, the spouse, the kids and work take priority, as they should.

Computer Work: The manipulation of a photo begins with the determination of what you are trying to accomplish. If your objective is to have a nice slide show at the end of the trip for your friends and family, the level of refinement is well within your reach on the first day. This initial approach is to load the images on the computer, march through them with two ideas; orientation [as you take the images in all sorts of strange orientations floating around your subjects] and deletions [for all those images that do not make the basic criteria – out of focus, can not recognize subject, "fish tails," or just plain dull]. On the Mac, there is a "easy button" for slide show where you can lay out the pictures, orient them correctly, select music [iTunes sounds or their basic selections], cut onto a DVD or CD, and store as a package for future showings. If you are on a PC, there are plenty of software packages that can be acquired to cut a beautiful Underwater Photo Safari onto a DVD for showing on TVs or computers. If you are after more complex outputs such as books or multi-media shows, there are plenty of programs that can take your pictures and present them in any manner you choose. The key is that you have the images from your Underwater Photo Safari stored and backed-up once you return home.

CHECKLIST FOR PHOTOGRAPHY PLANNING

The photographic equipment checklist is inserted inside the full checklist in the appendix and encompasses everything from batteries and lights to the actual cameras and all the associated backup items.

NOTES: _____

_____

_____

_____

CHAPTER 7: TRIP COMPLETION PREPARATION

The completion of an Underwater Photo Safari, either on a boat or land based, is a sad, sad affair. You must say goodbye to the people you dove with, the crew that supported you, and the locations you discovered. Most of us do not repeat complex international trips when there are so many new and exotic locations and so little time. Happiness is the realization that the friends you made can be inside your communications circles while the locations and adventures are recorded on you computer. Your trip ends in four phases that should be understood so that you can prepare for the post-trip emotional state and necessary actions. They are: departure, return activities, preparations for the next trip, and another adventure over the horizon.

True Blue Bay Resort Grenada Oct 2007
Pentax Optio S5i, 5 Meg Pix
Flash: off
Settings: auto
Distance: normal

DEPARTURE FROM THE BOAT

On the departure day of your Underwater Photo Safari, many things are going to happen. Preparation for this activity is important. Departure requires at least packing for the return, sharing email addresses, and setting up the post trip dive team meeting. One key element is to have your travel documents such as passports, airline reservations, hotel arrangements and phone numbers to call for pickup easily accessible. We usually sit in the room on the boat or at the hotel the night before departure and throw away all the spare paperwork from the trip. This lightens the tote bag you use for essentials during your travels. Coordination with the boat crew is fun with such issues as favorite recipes, exact dive locations and, of course, any payments due for items such as equipment rentals and, the every important, "crew tips." One nice activity that our dive team has fallen into is to search for and discover the items that the crew really has difficulty acquiring. This boat departure gift not only reflects our respect for the crew and how they treated us, but helps them operate in deployed locations. Some examples of practical gifts were:

In the Galapagos, a dive watch to a dive master
In the Bahamas, a new Harry Potter book 1 day after release
In Papua New Guinea, three dive knives and all our AA rechargeable batteries,
plus the charger.

In addition, as one leaves the boat, ensure that you have the "real" information on dive spots and times for your log book. The next table shows the dives over the week of the Grenada trip [we were on the Bago tender].

Dive Sites for Charter (13th – 20th October 2007)

	*	Dive #1	Dive #2	Dive #3	Dive #4	Dive #5
Sun	T	Ronde Reef	Diamond Rock	Sisters Slope		
	B	Frigate Rock	Sisters Slope	Diamond Rock	Isle de Ronde Reef	
Mon	T	Diamond Rock	Frigate Rock	Mabouya's Reef	Two Sisters	
	B	Diamond Rock	Mount de Caille	Two Sisters	Mabouya's Reef	
Tues	T	1st String Wall	North West Point	Boulders	Strattmann's Wreck	
	B	1st String Wall	Boulders	Simon's Surprise	North West Point	Strattmann's Wreck
Wed	T	West Wall	Devil's Table	Fish Mouth	Diver's Thirst	
	B	West Wall	Strattmans Wreck	Lireco	Herbie's Corner	
Thurs	T	Snake Channel	Garden Drift	Turtleback Drive		
	B	Myreau's Garden	Snake Channel	Mount de Caille	Sisters Cave	
Fri	T	Bianca 'C'	Purple Rain			
	B	Bianca 'C'	Purple Rain			

*Tender for boat: T is Trini & B is Bago

RETURN ACTIVITIES AND PLANNING

Return Activities and Planning are key elements of any adventure. You go to experience the new and remember the fun. After many trips I have come to believe the process, the travel and the experiences along the way are rewarding in and of themselves, as is, even, the return trip. This includes checking on the hotels, airline seats, and packing for airline weight restrictions.

Preparation for the return trip should have been accomplished in parallel with the outgoing portion of the adventure. However, on a live aboard Underwater Photo Safari, there are things you need to do as you leave the boat. The initial item is to check into the hotel (if you need to stay over a day as was required by the airlines for us in Grenada). This allows you to de-compress both physically and psychologically prior to charging back into the real world. A call home to confirm to the family that you are safe and sound is always appreciated. With this extra time, manipulation of the photos is usually our priority.

Grenada Sunset
Pentax Optio S5i,
5 megPix
Flash: auto
Settings: Auto

PREPARATIONS FOR THE NEXT TRIP

Preparation for the next trip puts a big red bow around your adventure once you get home. This includes all the follow-up action items such as putting the equipment away dry with one recurring thought -- when and where are we going on our next trip? After the successful completion of an Underwater Photo Safari, the feeling of excitement dies down and the realities of life sneak back into your consciousness. The necessary step of recording your trip loses its priority and the actual "cutting" of a DVD takes time and energy. A secret we have found is to plan a dive buddies trip party about three or four months after the actual excursion. This is an artificial deadline for all participants to have their photo's adjusted and DVD's cut. At the end of the previous trip one key to prepare for the next trip is to have the checklist revalidated by the review process:

- Did you take enough?
- Did you take too much?
- What steps should be added to the Step Zero Process?
- Did you forget to do anything?
- What would you do differently?

ANOTHER ADVENTURE OVER THE HORIZON

As we are all believers in a trip a year to keep the doctor away, the planning starts immediately upon return from one trip for the next. As soon as you are back, the excitement starts for another trip. The team must again start working on where and when to go on another Underwater Photo Safari. Indeed, we must start again at STEP ZERO.

CHECKLIST FOR COMPLETION PLANNING

Action Things to do at the END of the trip	**Completed**
-buy replacements and upgrade to better equipment	_____
-did you have all the correct power plugs	_____
-did you have all the correct diving papers, certification cards, visas, . . .	_____
-did you have enough cash money	_____
-did you have enough spare luggage to carry home all the things you bought	_____
-did your credit cards work	_____
-fix broken equipment	_____
-lessons learned, make a list of what went well and not so well so you can use it for your next trip	_____
-lessons learned, write them down	
-make a list of what you FORGOT and put it on your check list and lessons learned for next year.	_____
-make a list of what you took TOO much of, clothing, tools, cameras, electronics, paper, books, . . . and put in your check list and lessons learned for next year	_____
-make a trip book to show your friends, photos, videos, maps, tickets and such	_____
-make list of what broke and get it fixed	_____
-make list of what was used up and get more for next trip	_____
-replace lost/broken equipment	_____
-send "thank you" notes to boat crew, hotels and friends	_____

APPENDIX: UNDERWATER PHOTO SAFARI CHECKLIST

Note: *This list is written for those who will be traveling overseas but works well for those diving locally. An item may appear in more than one section because it is an important part of the system and the way we think. This list is for casual diving; however, a good starting point for Tech divers or those with rebreathers.*

The checklist is divided into two sections.

1. **ACTIONS** that you must accomplish and,
2. **EQUIPMENT**, a list of things to check and evaluate if you may need it on your trip.

The list has been sorted into *"a time zone"* where we recommend actions along with a space to indicate to record progress.

Time Zones

L = Long time prior to trip (12-6 months)
M = Medium time prior to trip (6-1 months)
S = short time prior to trip (1-4 weeks)

IMPORTANT - YOU MUST TAKE THESE FOLLOWING ITEMS!!!!!

Dive Documents
- DAN ID and Insurance card
- NITROX certification card
- Scuba diving certification card

Travel Documents
- Airline Tickets/travel vouchers
- Dive resort conformation numbers/emails/documents
- Drivers license
- Hotel conformation numbers/emails/documents
- Immunization certifications
- Medical insurance card(s)
- Passport
- Trip itinerary
- Visa(s)

Money
- Check book
- Credit cards (take more than one)
- Lots of cash in all size bills (don't rely on ATMs; but use ATMs if available)
- $100s, $50s, $20s, $10s, $1s (take a BUNCH of $1s for tips and small things) [if going overseas to a remote place, cash in lots of small bills is a must -- they don't make change there! At the airport exchange some of your larger bills into local currency to initially pay for cabs and tips.]

THESE ARE ACTIONS YOU MUST DO

Long-Term Actions	**Completed**
L arrange for vacation from work	_____
L luggage catch up days: add them to your travel plan, some luggage will get lost on the airlines. A rest day will give it a chance to catch up with you.	_____
L make airline reservations	_____
L make hotel reservations	_____
L make dive resort reservations	
L passport expiration date; check it and ensure you will have at least 6 months left when you enter your vacation area, more is better	_____
L read lessons learned from your last trip	_____
L rest days, put them in your travel plan. This will give your body a chance to catch up and for you to see the local area and enjoy your trip	_____

L   time zones, do you cross the international date line,   _____
     watch this, you can loose or gain one day; this
     can screw up your travel plans if you don't double check.

L   Dive trip planning parties; get together with friends   _____
     and discuss going on a trip; interim team parties
     will check individual progress and provide group support

Medium-Term Actions

M   arrange for animals/pets/lawn/flowers   _____

M   boat, will diving be from small tenders   _____

M   boat, will there be a camera table and rinse tank   _____

M   boat, will there be a changing room and bathroom (head)   _____

M   charge rechargeable batteries prior to trip; let them sit   _____
     for 20 days test and check for batteries that have
     discharged; indicates a week battery; toss it out.

M   check all O-rings on lights and cameras (take lots of   _____
     spares, they are light)

M   check your electrical devices to see if they are compatible   _____
     with the electricity in the area you are going to or transiting

M   customs and import restrictions, understand what they are   _____
     and be ready to comply

M   dive trip planning parties; get together and check individual   _____
     progress. This will provide support and motivation for
     getting things done.

M   diving conditions, will we be doing shore diving   _____

M   diving conditions, read the reviews in magazines and the   _____
     on-line news groups

M   diving conditions, what is the water temperature, do I need   _____
     a wetsuit, the thickness of our hood, gloves, and wetsuit

M   diving conditions, will be doing shallow, wall, reef or wreck   _____
     diving

M   diving conditions, will the current be still or strong drift diving   _____

M diving conditions, will the seas be rough open water or calm, _____
sheltered diving

M diving equipment rentals, does the dive shop rent _____
equipment, do you need to reserve it

M diving level, what skill level is required, beginner, _____
intermediate, experienced, or professional

M diving, are there training courses I can take _____

M diving, are there training courses I need _____

M electrical voltage and wall plug design for each country and _____
ship you will visit or be on; it may change in the same
country - find out what they are and read the power supply on
your equipment; will it work; do I need a plug adaptor/converter

M entertainment in the local area, tours, shopping, museums, _____
parks, music, food, farming, golf, site seeing; get out and see
the local area

M get Divers Alert Network (DAN) scuba diving insurance _____

M get necessary shots/vaccinations/prescriptions (malaria, _____
tetanus, Hep A&B, polio . . .)

M have regulator serviced _____

M insurance, do get overseas medical, scuba diving and _____
medical evacuation insurance

M insurance, should I get lost luggage or canceled trip _____
Insurance

M local area, maps, get maps of where you are going; will _____
greatly improve your enjoyment knowing where you are
going and have been.

M local history and culture, buy books and read them. You _____
will enjoy a lot more of what you see on the trip

M local reputation of tour organization/hotel/resort/dive outfits, _____
what is their reputation? Check on line and in magazines

M luggage size restrictions, if you bag is too big, you will have _____
to check it. Many small airlines (island hoppers) have almost
no overhead storage.

M make copy of medical prescriptions (take with you)   _____

M make copy of optical prescription (take with you)   _____

M make list of contact phone numbers you may need to call   _____
(family, friends and work to tell them you may be late
returning)

M reconfirm all hotel reservations   _____

M reconfirm all resort reservations   _____

M reconfirm dive operation arrangements   _____

M safety, what are the local diving safety requirement,   _____
do you need special equipment

M test all lights   _____

M test regulator on spare tank

Short-Term Actions

S alcohol, tobacco, foods, what products can you take into or   _____
out the places you will visit

S call credit card companies, tell them you are going   _____
overseas so they may adjust your spending profile

S check dive computer battery and change if you have doubt   _____

S diving gas, does the resort have NITROX   _____

S fishing restrictions, what can you do in the vacation area,
pole fishing, spear fishing or none

S food and organic products, what can you take into or out of   _____
the places you will visit

S food, tell the resorts if you have any special food or   _____
dietary needs

S get necessary pills (prescriptions, over the counter,   _____
malaria, vitamins, . .)

S internet, is there internet in your vacation area at the   _____
hotel/resort/café so you may send emails to your friends at
work and tell them how much fun you are having on vacation

S label everything; keeps it from getting mixed up on boat   _____

S   lay out all dive equipment from head to foot to make certain   _____
     you have it all prior to packing

S   lay out camera equipment in its proper place to make   _____
     certain you have it all; also good to hook it all up and check
     operation.

S   luggage, mark luggage with colored tape or string; makes it   _____
     easy to find in the airport and hotel

S   luggage, put two name tags on each piece, they tend to get   _____
     ripped off

S   make copies of your Cert-cards, passport, visas and other   _____
     papers (swap with travel buddy)

S   money in local area; what kind do they use, how do you   _____
     convert, do they have ATMs, WHERE can you do it, do they
     take credit cards

S   pack everything in plastic bags, keeps it dry and easy to sort _____

S   pets, arrange for someone to take care of them or take them _____
     to a pet boarding facility

S   phone numbers and emails where you will be, make a list   _____
     and give to your family and friends at home so they can
     contact you

S   phone numbers and emails, make a list of them for the   _____
     resorts and tour companies you are going to visit so you can
     take on trip

S   phone numbers and emails, make a list of the folks at home _____
     so you can call them

S   phone service in your vacation area, is there service,   _____
     (in some remote areas, there is NO phone service)

S   phone service, will your cell phone work in the vacation area _____

S   plants, arrange for someone to take care of your plants   _____

S   plants, what can you take into or out of the places you visit _____

S   reconfirm all airline reservations and seat assignments   _____

S   refill medical prescriptions (we cannot stress this enough)   _____

S   reconfirm all hotel reservations   _____

S reconfirm all resort reservations   _____

S reconfirm dive operation arrangements   _____

S smoking restrictions, what are the guidelines for the hotels,   _____
resorts, and dive boats you will visiting/using/staying on

S smoking restrictions, will you be traveling with smokers or   _____
non-smokers - be considerate

S smoking, what tobacco can you take into or out of the places   _____
you will visit

S sharpen all knifes and lightly coat with oil   _____

S State Department, check their web site for current   _____
information on the local political situation

S State Department, get location and contact information for   _____
the local US Embassy services

S State Department, register your overseas trip with State   _____
Department, important for remote and unstable political areas

S stop home snail mail, newspapers and deliveries   _____

S tell neighbors you are going, AGAIN, give them your contact   _____
info, get/verify their contact info

S tipping expectations, research what is expected, what is too   _____
much, what is the norm, how do you tip, what currency do
you use, can you use credit cards

S write down credit card numbers and international phone   _____
numbers for each company

S weigh luggage; repack or toss out stuff if your bags   _____
are too heavy

S take copies of the wavers you sent in advance and   _____
give to boat (this will save you from filling them out again,
forms tend to get lost)

S go to your luggage pile and toss out 10 pounds, you   _____
packed too much!!!

S diver certification cards; DO YOU HAVE THEM!!   _____

ACTION THINGS TO DO ON THE TRIP   **Completed**

call your dive tour company and let them know you   _____
        have arrived in the vacation area and will be at the
        appropriate location for pick up as scheduled.
buy things for your trip book; maps, photos & postcards   _____
get list of your dive sites   _____
get list of the passengers on your dive boat, resort   _____
        and hotels
keep activity list and opinions for reference at the end of the   _____
        cruse/stay when you write the performance critique/
        feedback for the boat/hotel, good feedback is also needed
make list of things you need for your next trip   _____
notify your home family/neighbors of your travel &
progress of your trip; they want to know you are ok
purchases, make list of what you buy so you can put on   _____
        customs list when you reenter the US *(see US Customs*
        and Boarder Protection CBP Publicaion No. 0000-00512)
start lessons learned list   _____

ACTION THINGS TO DO AT THE END OF THE TRIP   **COMPLETED**

buy replacement or upgrade to better equipment   _____
did you have all the correct power plugs   _____
did you have all the correct diving papers, certification   _____
        cards, visas, . . .
did you have enough cash   _____
did you have enough spare luggage to carry home all the   _____
        things you bought
did your credit cards work   _____
fix broken equipment   _____

lessons learned, make a list of what went well and not so well   _____
    so you can use it for your next trip

lessons learned, write them down

make a list of what you FORGOT and put it on your check list   _____
    and lessons learned for next year.

make a list of what you took TOO much of, clothing, tools,   _____
    cameras, electronics, paper, books, . . . and put in your
    check list and lessons learned for next year

make a trip book to show your friends, photos, videos, maps,   _____
    tickets and such

make list of what broke and get it fixed   _____

make list of what was used up and get more for next trip   _____

replace lost/broken equipment   _____

send "thank you" notes to boat crew, hotels and friends you   _____
    made on the trip

ACTION THINGS TO NOT TAKE ON THE TRIP   **Completed**

illegal drugs with you; foreign laws are very tough and the   _____
    jails are not nice

scuba tanks, they are very heavy and provided by most scuba   _____
    operations as part of your dive charter

weights, they are very heavy and provided by most scuba   _____
    operations as part of your dive charter

heavy books, take paperbacks and swap books with others   _____
    on the trip; use the local take one, leave one library

food, most items are prohibited and are seized at customs when
    entering a country, buy local; remember, you are on   _____
    an adventure

too many clothes; use items that can be cleaned in your room   _____
    on the trip or use hotel laundry

large containers of liquids; they are heavy, use travel sizes or   _____
    buy locally

you may want to rent regulators or BCs from your dive   _____
    operation; saves a LOT of luggage weight.

NOTES: _____

_____

_____

_____

EQUIPMENT CHECK LIST

The list is segmented by the type of equipment and by time frame. Many of the items require significant lead time to acquire. Go get them or locate them in your house and put them into a "take on the trip pile" early. Yep, a "pile" may sound stupid but it works. Put everything you want to take into one, out of the way place and keep adding to it so you won't forget anything.

DIVE EQUIPMENT

Basic Equipment
_____**M**-buoyancy compensation device

_____**M**-dive bag, mesh for carrying all this stuff onto the boat

_____**M**-dive boots

_____**M**-dive computer

_____**M**-dive knife

_____**M**-dive log book with sufficient blank pages

_____**M**-dive mask

_____**M**-dry bag for keeping your dry towel and shirt

_____**M**-ear wash

_____M-fins

_____M-mask defog solution

_____M-regulator with submersible pressure gauge and octopus

_____M-retractors for small equipment (lights and such)

_____M-save-a-dive kit (spare mask strap, fin strap, regulator mouthpiece)

_____M-snorkel

_____M-strong plastic box to put your eyeglasses and such into while you are diving; keeps them from getting broken or lost

_____M-custom, padded weight belt (the boat will provide standard belts)

_____M-wet suit (two are better, one warm and one warmer; vest, shorty)

_____M-white electrical tape and marking pen to mark equipment

SAFETY EQUIPMENT

_____M-chemical/cyalume light stick

_____M-dive alert air horn (connects to the regulator, very loud)

_____M-Divers Alert Network (DAN) scuba diving insurance

_____M-travel insurance

_____M-inflatable safety sausage (easy to see you from the boat)

_____M-signaling mirror and whistle

_____M-UW strobe light for personal use

Backup Equipment

_____M-booties

_____M-dive light

_____M-2nd dive knife

_____M-dive slate

_____M-2nd dry box/bag

_____M-fins

_____M-gloves

_____M-hose clips, to attach hoses to BC

_____M-mask (really consider this, masks are really personal)

_____M-octo regulator keepers

_____ **M**-regulator

_____ **M**-stainless steel clip rings

PHOTOGRAPHY

Land Camera (are you going to take one)

_____ **M**-batteries w/extra

_____ **M**-charger for land camera battery

_____ **M**-extra lenses (wide angle/telephoto)

_____ **M**-land camera, prime use

_____ **M**-land camera, spare use

_____ **S**-air blower for cleaning camera

_____ **S**-camera brush

_____ **S**-lens caps

_____ **S**-lens filters (polarizer, UV filter, neutral density and such)

_____ **S**-lens hoods

_____ **S**-lens cleaning paper

_____ **S**-micro fiber towel

Under Water (UW) camera (are you going to take one)

_____ **M**-batteries w/extra

_____ **M**-charger for UW camera battery

_____ **M**-desiccant packs

_____ **M**-extra lenses (wide angle/macro)

_____ **M**-UW camera, prime use

_____ **M**-UW camera, spare use

_____ **M**-UW camera housing, prime use

_____ **M**-UW camera housing, spare use

_____ **M**-UW focus/modeling light

_____ **M**-UW strobes with cords

_____ **M**-UW strobe arms

LIGHTS

_____**M**-batteries for all lights (count and check size for what you need)

_____**M**-dive lights (prime, small, backup)

_____**M**-small flashlight for searching in carry-on bag

_____**M**-small light for room/ night light

_____**M**-spare bulbs for all lights

_____**M**-UW strobe light

_____**M**-UW tank marker light

_____**S**-extra batteries

_____**S**-extra lights

_____**S**-extra O-rings for lights

BATTERIES

_____**M**-batteries for all cameras (determine sizes and number needed)

_____**M**-batteries for all lights (determine sizes and number needed)

_____**M**-batteries for noise reduction headphones for flights

_____**M**-batteries for cell phone [+ charger]

_____**M**-batteries for GPS

_____**M**-battery tester (a good cheap $ 5 tester from Radio Shack works fine)

_____**M**-extra batteries (all needed sizes)

_____**M**-extra batteries for all dive computers

TOOLS

Repair Tools

_____**M**-crescent wrench

_____**M**-dental tape and large needles for sewing

_____**M**-double end brass clip

_____**M**-duct tape

_____**M**-extra burst-plus for tanks (unique item, not needed in most places)

_____**M**-flame maker for burning end of nylon cords (don't take on
 plane/ buy at location)

_____**M**-knife sharpening tool/stone

_____**M**-leather man tool

_____**M**-multi-purpose dive tool

_____**M**-nylon cables ties, small and large (zip ties)

_____**M**-plastic bags, several sizes

_____**M**-rubber bands

_____**M**-rubberized repair tape

_____**M**-screwdrivers, several sizes and very small (for photo equipment)

_____**M**-screwdrivers (blade, philips and terex)

_____**M**-single edge razor blades for cutting equipment

_____**M**-small battery tester

_____**M**-small, medium, large bungee cords

_____**M**-spare low/high pressure plugs for regulator 1st stage, wrenches to fit

_____**M**-spare low/high pressure swivels for regulator

_____**M**-super glue

_____**M**-surgical tubing

_____**M**-swiss army knife

_____**M**-tire patch kit to fix BCD

_____**M**-velcro ties

_____**M**-WD-40, small, don't take on airplane, by at location

_____**S**-plastic bags to put things in; keeps stuff from getting tangled/lost/wet

O-rings [light, so carry many spares]

_____**M**-extra O-rings for everything (lights, camera, strobe sync
 cables, regularor, LP and HP connector hoses, tank O-rings)

_____**M**-extra O-rings for UW camera housings

_____**M**-silicone grease for O-rings, watch manufactures recommendations

_____**M**-metal dental tooth scraper tool fo extracting tough O-rings

_____**M**-plastic O-ring tool to get O-rings off and out of equipment

_____**S**-swabs

BOOKS & OWNER'S MANUALS

_____**M**-most manuals are available in electronic formant
_____**M**-put them on your computer, it saves space and weight
_____**M**-Air/NITROX tables
_____**M**-area travel & tourist books
_____**M**-camera owner's manual
_____**M**-dive computer owner's manual (this is IMPORTANT)
_____**M**-fish ID books (the boat usually has a good set)
_____**M**-GPS owner's manual
_____**M**-how to books for (photography, fish ID, bird ID, . . .)
_____**M**-maps
_____**M**-owner's manual for EVERYTHING you take
_____**M**-UW strobe owner's manual
_____**M**-UW and land camera owner's manual

FIRST AID KIT

_____**S**-alcohol wash for ears
_____**S**-antiseptic cream/lotion
_____**S**-anti-sting lotion for sea urchin and jelly fish stings
_____**S**-aspirin and other pain relievers
_____**S**-band aids
_____**S**-bug spray
_____**S**-cough drops
_____**S**-decongestant
_____**S**-pooper starter
_____**S**-pooper stopper
_____**S**-sunscreen

MEDICAL AND PERSONAL HEALTH

_____ **M**-determine surface and water temperature where you are
      going (determines wet suit needs)

_____ **M**-determine altitude at which you will be diving, sea level or
      mountain lake (determines decompression constraints)

_____ **M**-special medical equipment (parts for prosthetic limbs, . .)

_____ **M**-diabetes blood/sugar test equipment

_____ **M**-get divers Alert Network (DAN) scuba diving medical insurance

_____ **M**-get physical certifying you to scuba dive

_____ **M**-get travel insurance for delays, lost luggage, . . .

_____ **M**-malaria pills if required

_____ **M**-special inoculations for area you are going

_____ **M**-prescription medications for duration of trip THIS IS IMPORTANT

_____ **M**-copies of written prescription to show customs

_____ **M**-feminine hygiene products are not readily available everywhere

_____ **S**-antibacterial wipes

_____ **S**-dental hygiene (tooth brush/paste, floss, picks, mouth wash . .)

_____ **S**-deodorant

_____ **S**-diabetes blood sugar test kit

_____ **S**-fungus lotions

_____ **S**-hand cream/lotion

_____ **S**-non-prescription medications

_____ **S**-prescription medications for duration of trip THIS IS IMPORTANT

_____ **S**-copies of written prescription to show customs

_____ **S**-razor and shaving cream

_____ **S**-washing lotions for body and clothes

_____ **S**-bug spray

_____ **S**-sun glasses, polarized, reduces water glare

_____ **S**-suntan lotion

_____ **S**-sea sick pills

_____ **S**-chap stick

CLOTHING

_____M-plastic bags, for clothes - keeps them dry and clean/dirty
_____S-bathing suit(s)
_____S-beach robe/skirt
_____S-blouses/shirts
_____S-clothesline and clips (make out of nylon cord and two carabineers
        for use on boat dive deck, hang bathing suits to day)
_____S-hat, with chin strap so it won't blow off, needed for sun
_____S-polo shirt
_____S-sandals
_____S-shorts
_____S-skirt
_____S-socks
_____S-tennis shoes
_____S-trousers
_____S-T-shirts
_____S-underclothing

PERSONAL ITEMS

_____M-contacts + extra pair of contacts
_____M-eye glasses + extra pair
_____M-sun glasses
_____M-extra pair of sun glasses
_____M-reading glasses
_____M-TSA approved locks for checked and hand luggage & photo cases
_____S-binoculars
_____S-business cards
_____S-small travel alarm clock for room
_____S-contact solution and case
_____S-DVDs to watch
_____S-extra luggage bag for taking things home

_____ S-hair bands
_____ S-pens, pencils and paper
_____ S-reading material (try to buy/exchange locally, saves weight)
_____ S-sewing kit with needle and various threads
_____ S-big needle and carpet thread for sewing equipment
_____ S-tote bags, small and large

PERSONAL COMPUTER

_____ M-computer for processing photos, email, watching movies,
          writing notes, keeping a dive log, logging GPS data of your dive sites
_____ M-computer battery charger
_____ M-external HD for backing up computer data
_____ M-camera memory card reader
_____ M-several thumb drives
_____ M-software (SW) for burning CDs and DVDs
_____ M-SW for sending emails
_____ M-SW for processing photos
_____ M-SW for word processing
_____ S-blank CDs and DVDs
_____ S-CD/DVD protector sleeves
_____ S-pen to write on CDs and DVDs

OTHER PERSONAL ELECTRONICS

_____ M-cables for computer, iPod and camera to display photos/video on TV
_____ M-cables to connect all your things together
_____ M-cell phone w/authorization for international calls & charger
_____ M-chase down the access codes to make calls from foreign locations
_____ M-battery chargers for everything electronic
_____ M-external speaker for computer/iPod; makes room listening easier
_____ M-iPod with charger
_____ M-PDA with security protection

_____**M**-satellite telephone with charger

_____**M**-short wave radio; excellent for current events in remote locations

_____**S**-access codes for telephones in the countries you visit

_____**S**-ear bud headphones

_____**S**-electrical plug style adaptor so you can plug in at travel location

_____**S**-extension cords (one for battery charging station and one for room) that are thin, light and have multiple plug openings

_____**S**-flashlight and night light for room

_____**S**-GPS to plot and record travel locations and dive sites

_____**S**-noise reduction headphones (great for very long airplane trips)

LaVergne, TN USA
29 October 2009
162475LV00002B